I WAS AN
Awesomer
KID

Brad Getty

CHRONICLE BOOKS

SAN FRANCISCO

Text copyright © 2015 by Brad Getty.

Cover photograph © Lane Jordan. Used with permission.
Cover model: Lane Jordan

All rights reserved. No part of this book may be reproduced in any
form without written permission from the publisher.

Library of Congress Cataloging-in-Publication Data:

Getty, Brad.
  I was an awesomer kid / Brad Getty.
    pages cm
  ISBN 978-1-4521-3653-0
1. Children—Humor. I. Title.

  PN6231.C32G48 2015
  818'.602—dc23

                                    2014034710

Manufactured in China

Designed by Nami Kurita and Allison Weiner

10 9 8 7 6 5 4 3 2 1

Chronicle Books LLC
680 Second Street
San Francisco, California 94107
www.chroniclebooks.com

"Adults are just obsolete children
and the hell with them."
—DR. SEUSS

INTRODUCTION

Back when skinned knees and grass stains were your badges of honor, you were a death-dodging Picasso of finger painting who pissed into the wind of life . . . and your pants.

Your imagination ran wild and you ran wilder. You were free, you were crazy, you were terrible, you were an awesomer kid.

YOUR ATTITUDE WAS AWESOMER

You were the biggest little badass this world had ever seen. Fear feared you as you rolled through the streets with training wheels and a ten-foot-tall swagger. If you could count, you'd count all the shits you didn't give. Some called it the terrible twos, but that was just you asserting your undersized self in an oversized world.

GOING FOR IT

You risked it all and then some. Broken bones and endless doctor bills were your calling cards as you crashed through your existence. Adrenaline was your drug, speed was your muse, and death was your copilot. Every day was another chance to reach for the danger zone and risk your life in the pursuit of badassness.

Now you overanalyze risk and carefully walk the tightrope of safety. You live in an airbag-filled world.

Let's feel alive again. Safe is boring. Let's raise hell and the hair on the back of our necks again like when we were awesomer kids.

Olympians had nothing on you, so you shut down the show by killing your living-room-floor routine that ended with your signature London Bridge splits. Every public outing was your chance to claim fifteen minutes of fame, and each performance fearlessly began with "Look at what I can do!"

Now you're terrified to display your God-given talents. Your brain whispers lies to your confidence that keep you out of the spotlight. "You're not good enough." "They'll make fun of you." "You shouldn't do this at a wedding reception."

Screw that. Stop doubting yourself. It's time to show off the way you did when you were an awesomer kid.

YOUR WAY OR NO WAY

Long before you skulled two beers to the face, you were straight double-crushing bottles of juice . . . and life.

So, next time you're saddled up to two fists full of the frost-brewed finest, cheers yourself for inventing the most awesome way to drink.

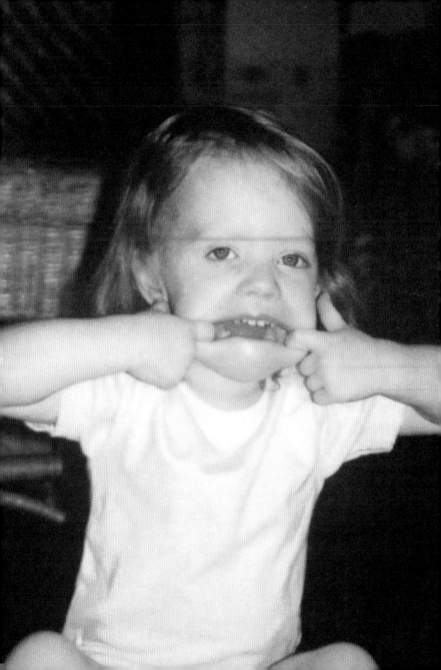

ALTERNATE REALITIES

Your think-box was still untamed by school. Mind-expanding drugs couldn't help adults reach the far-off places your mind created. Dragon rides, imaginary friends, and ninja underwear fights were completely normal.

Now you've got the imagination of a rock. You can't even finger paint an animal that has never existed or make up a planet in outer space.

It's bullshit. Let's daydream again. Let's make believe and believe in what we've made up.

MONSTER FACES

Only suckers smile. When the camera came out you performed facial gymnastics and contorted your cute little looks into monstrous configurations. Each new vanguard expression was conjured from the inner demon that you were.

Now, you put on your best face for the world because you care about its opinion. Each carefully practiced smile is an attempt to trick everyone into believing that you're a happy, well-adjusted, socially acceptable adult.

But fake smiles are boring. Let's make faces for fun again and shock the world with our weirdness like an awesomer kid would.

ANYTHING'S A TOY

Maybe it was that hit to the soft spot, but you found endless fun everywhere. You'd stack cans for hours and laugh at your nose getting stolen.

Now you're bored even with 487 TV channels. Internet has rotted your brain and social media makes you less social. You're bored because you're boring.

Let's wean ourselves from the screen. Let's look at everything as a toy and make up games that the world has never played. Let's log off-line and log back into life like when we were awesomer.

NOT SHARING THE SPOTLIGHT

It was your thunder and nobody was going to steal it. So you shoved snotnoses out of your moments because your stage wasn't meant to be shared.

It's a bullshit world now where everyone gets their time to shine. Participant ribbons have taken the place of first-place trophies and everyone is a star.

It's time to stop sharing and worrying about everyone's "feelings." If we work our asses off, we take the credit. Life is a fight and the people who win it should just enjoy the glory like an awesomer kid would.

ORIGINAL JACKASS

You were a goofy bastard whose oddball antics kept everyone entertained. What few thoughts went through your brain usually resulted in unintentional comedic gold that went down in family history. You were the jackass before Jackass ever started getting hit in the nuts for TV.

Now you worry about how you'll be perceived. Your business life has spilled into the off hours and every social-media interaction is polished to present you in your best light.

Seriously, let's be less serious again. We're all different shades of strange and it's time to stop hiding the amazing offbeat awesomer kid that is in all of us.

INDEPENDENCE

Child leashes were a response to your lone-wolf ways. Your wild spirit called you to wander and venture away from the pack until mall security picked you up.

You never strike out on your own now. You surround yourself with people because society has told you that loners are losers.

We don't need anyone else. Let's see movies alone, get dinner by ourselves, and have a drink with us. The leash is gone, so let's get lost again and leave our footprints around the globe like our awesomer kid always wanted to.

Before you ever learned to eat your feelings, you flew a finger salute in the air and let the world know how you really felt. Your aunt knew she looked fat in those pants and you didn't feel sorry for saying it.

Now you hide behind a veneer of niceties as you lie your way through each day. You're living an "okay" life in a world where the "crazy" label is quickly applied to anyone who steps outside the preapproved decibel level of emotion.

Screw that. Let's get angry again . . . and sad, and happy, and goofy. Let's show how we really feel, and live honestly like we did when we were awesomer kids.

NO CONCEPT OF MONEY

You didn't know what poor was. Your brain used its MacGyver skills to dream up what you didn't have. Sticks were imaginary swords, boxes could take you to outer space, and sliced bread could be a birthday cake. You invented your own type of richness not based on cash rules.

You do it for the dollar now. From the moment you rise to the second you fall asleep you chase the carrot of wealth.

But let's not spend our whole lives spending. Let's work with what we've got and be happy anyway, just like we did when we were awesomer kids.

DISRUPTING THE PEACE

You sucker punched the world with your antics. You were the loud armpit fart in church, the yellow name written in the snow, and the stink bomb in class. Nobody was safe from you . . . ever.

You're timid now. Instead of disrupting the peace with your comedic gold, you quietly help keep it.

It's time to get wild again, pull pranks, and stir things up. Let's do something so unexpected that people would only expect it from an awesomer kid, which you used to be.

HATIN' STUFF

Screw brussels sprouts. Green beans could kiss your baby-powdered ass, and anything that wasn't sugar-coated could eat itself. It was a black-and-white kind of world divided into gross stuff and good stuff. You weren't going to waste your baby teeth on anything that wouldn't rot them out.

Now you choke down vegetables that you once fed the dog and make food you would have spit into a napkin. Healthy labels are an excuse for food to taste like crap.

Nope. Don't do it. Throw down your fork and stand up for your taste buds. Let's go back to loving what we love, hating what we hate, and enjoying every damn bite we take out of life.

BEING YOUR OWN STUNT MAN

Evel Knievel had to start somewhere. So, you pulled up your Huggies and went all balls at mad two-inch jumps. You were on the road to badassery and destined for destruction.

You're a risk faker now. You've derailed your crash course of life and chosen the safe road everyone travels.

Let's roll the dice again. Let's break new ground and show the world we still have the balls to go after it.

No kid ever said they wanted to be an adult when they grew up.

Each day you saddled up to life like a pint-sized daredevil and challenged fate to erase your existence. "Baby proofing" was a polite name for "death proofing" because electrical outlets were just as good as best friends and hot stoves needed to be touched. You didn't know you could die, which gave you the freedom to live so hard.

Now, you're a terrified sissy. You eat healthy, quit smoking, stopped drinking, don't speed, get regular checkups, work out, wear sunscreen, avoid sugar, and reduce your existence to just trying to avoid death.

We can't escape our fates. So why not embrace our mortality and party our way into the grave like awesomer kids?

CREATIVE SOLUTIONS

Underestimated in both size and genius, you dared to dream of the uninvented. Instead of roasting your marshmallows with a bent coat hanger, you invented a dragon-tamer technique and next-leveled your s'more game. You had a solution to all of life's problems and proto-typed your dreams in Legos.

Now the system has beaten you dull. You think inside the rules and march to the same beat as everyone else.

Let's forget how things are supposed to be done and start doing them our way again. Let's create the solutions boring brains can't even imagine and do things the awesomer way.

NO INSIDE VOICE

There was going to be hell if you weren't heard. You didn't just break the silence, you shattered it with a howl and made sure everyone's ears rang with your demands. There was never a question of what you wanted, because even the neighbors could hear you asking for it.

The power you projected from your lungs is gone now. You're the world's doormat and it wipes its feet on you because your timid whispers don't command authority.

Let's get our roar back. Let's shake rooms with our voices. Inside voices are bullshit; we're going to use our awesomer ones instead.

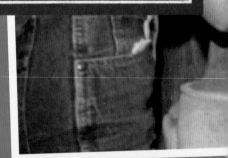

NOT UNDERSTANDING LIFE

Talking boxes? Moving pictures? Getting your nose stolen? It was a hard-knock life back then because your mind was being blown faster than you could figure anything out. You nearly shit yourself the first time you saw your reflection and again when your people disappeared during peekaboo.

Now you stay comfortably in your little bubble of knowledge. You don't want to put yourself in situations where you're going to feel like a moron. You shy away from the new and different.

Let's feel dumb again. Let's seek out things we don't understand and try things we don't know how to do.

BEING A WILD CARD

Your brain functioned in ways doctors feared. It was a collider of random ideas that mixed the world up in ways that had never been seen. ADD was the only inventable explanation for your hyperactive antics.

The doctors have dosed you with a cocktail of calm now. You've quietly let yourself slip into the square hole of society and fallen in the trap of being normal.

But the world needs crazy. Without our spark of spontaneity, each day rolls into the next as we march our way through days like drones. Screw being a copy of a copy, let's get back to being our own brand of crazy.

HAVING SWAGGER

When you weren't rolling through the streets with sippy-cup confidence, you were locking down the playground like a straight Pampers pimp. You were the definition of badass-cute and always dressed to impress . . . even if you couldn't dress yourself.

Now you've got no attitude in your steps and no style in your slacks. Your closet is a corporate filing cabinet of beige colors and golf outfits.

So let's make a statement again. Wear what we love and own it—who cares if it matches?

You literally had your whole life ahead of you. Each tomorrow felt forever away so you carpe-diemed the shit out of existence. There was no five-year plan. Hell, you barely had a five-minute plan.

Adult problems rule your life now. You live in the "nexts"—next day, next week, next month, next year. You're planning a life instead of living it.

Let's get back to be awesomer by forgetting that the future will ever arrive.

BEING A BADASS

Dora the Explorer was nothing compared to you. Your death-dodging, danger-chasing spirit led you to the mountaintop of living.

You climb corporate ladders instead of mountains now. The ends of the earth don't compel your soul to see them because you've landed comfortably into an ergonomic chair.

Instead of working for a living, we should work so that we can start living. Let's be king of the mountain of kicking ass again.

GETTIN' BACK UP

You were a walking fail-montage of catastrophic self-injury. You spent the formative years of your life picking yourself off the ground and learned more from your mistakes than from anything you were taught.

You fear failing now. You never get knocked down because you never take the risks that will put you in the record books.

Let's try stuff we've never done and fall on our faces doing it. Let's get knocked down, then get back up and do it again 'til we get it right.

UNEXPLAINABLE SITUATIONS

You were the Einstein of inventing trouble. You could turn the simplest household items into death contraptions which you experimented with on your siblings. Your antics drove the pets away and grayed your parents' dark locks with every inconceivable thing they found you doing.

You're a trustworthy old sack of bones now. Nobody fears coming home to the destruction you might cause because most likely all you did was nap.

Let's get back to our roots of raising hell. Let's be the wild card everyone feared, just like when we were awesomer kids.

The best adults are the ones who stayed weird kids.

BEING COOL

There's a reason people say "cool kid" and not "cool adult" and it was you. You were King Shit of the playground and the freshest thing since baby powder.

You're lame sauce now. You're following trends instead of setting them.

Let's be the coolest people we know again. Let's only do stuff that rules and flash middle fingers as deuces to anyone who doesn't like it.

DOING IT YOUR WAY

Your undereducated intelligence made your mind a Swiss army knife at solving life. Instead of being blinded by the crutch of knowledge, you used your IQ to baby-Einstein a fresh perspective. There was a right way, a wrong way, and your way.

Now you're a directions follower. You're tits on a bull if someone isn't telling you how to do something.

Let's find our own way again. Edison didn't ask how to make the light-bulb, he just made it. Let's solve problems in the way only we can . . . by being awesomer. Sprinkler washing machine? Why not?

Age is a number, young is a feeling. Stay awesomer.

BEING A MAVERICK

Temper tantrums? No, those were forceful revolts against the unjust rules being applied to you by a governing body you didn't choose. Each insurrection against nap time, sharing, healthy green bullshit, and wearing clothes in photos was you marking your line in the sand.

You've lost your backbone now. Did you become illiterate in the art of standing up for yourself? Standing up for anything?

Let's start a revolution and flash a bare ass at growing old. Let's live our way or no way.

PISSING OFF THE WORLD

You were the original Dennis the Menace, tormenting the world with your antics. Matches, plastic bags, and spray paint now carry warning labels because of what you did with them. Every wrinkle on your parents' faces could be counted against some catastrophic event you had caused and 911 knew you by name.

Now your only behavior is good. Your conscience is driving the car and the angel on your shoulder is giving all the directions.

Let's listen to the devil on our other shoulder again. Let's find that spark of mischief and stir up some shenanigans before it's too late.

SUCKING AT STUFF

The first dozen or so years of your life were filled with reckless experimentation. You struck out at tee ball, failed at soccer, and had two left feet. But you always got back up because you knew you were God's gift to something . . . even if you hadn't figured it out yet.

You're cool with the skills you've got now. Good is good enough and you'd rather make fun of people who face-plant while trying to become living legends than attempt something new.

Let's be failures again. Let's do stuff we suck at and work our asses off to get better. Let's become awesomer kids with the maddest skillz this earth has ever seen.

The world had never seen a skateboarding paleontologist, but you were determined to kick-flip your way into history . . . and over T. rex. Guidance counselors and college could kiss your baby-smooth ass because your aptitude was an appetite for destruction. Every day you'd change jobs with the wind and go from riding on garbage trucks to being a cowboy of space.

You're caged in a cubicle now where your life is an endless spreadsheet nightmare. You've got Microsoft Office dreams in a PowerPoint-driven life.

Let's end our nine-to-five misery. Let's dare to live our passions. Suits are for suckers, which is why no awesomer kid ever said he wanted to be a banker.

NOT EASILY IMPRESSED

How could you be impressed with the mundane day-to-day living of a regular life? You watched cars transform into robots and were raised to believe that a fat man could slide down your chimney just to give you gifts. The bar for your expectations was set too high since birth because you were raised with the world revolving around you.

Some gold doesn't always stay gold and some things just can't stay awesomer. Sorry.

Cool kids never die. Boring adults never live.

BEING WEIRD

Normal to you was eating crayons and washing them down with paste. It was wearing underwear over your pants and pretending to fly across the living room. Your best friend was imaginary and you wore eyes over your eyes so people wouldn't know where you were really looking.

Now you've learned to quietly suppress your oddness because society labels those it doesn't understand as "freaks."

Screw that. We're all odd in our own ways, so let's be freaks—together. After all, the weirder we are the awesomer we get.

NOT GIVING TWO SHITS

You couldn't count all the shits you didn't give, but that was mostly because you couldn't count. If you got tired, you'd sit wherever you were and then not give a shit that people were judging you, not give a shit that they had to walk around you, and most important, not give a shit that your parents were getting judged by other parents.

You give so many shits now that your hair is falling out from stress and you can't sleep at night. You care what your neighbors think. You worry about how your coworkers react.

Screw 'em. Let's go back to it being our way or no way. Let's be awesomer and take a seat in the street of life.

BEING GULLIBLE

Your world was a beautiful lie where a fat man delivered gifts if you were "good" and a fairy wanted to give you money for your rotten teeth. Your parents laughed each night as they thought back to the wildly ridiculous things they convinced you were real.

You know *gullible* is in the dictionary now, because you looked it up. And the complex deceptions you've survived in your younger life have made you skeptical of everyone.

But let's restore some faith in humanity. Let's believe in what people say instead of rushing to Google to prove everyone wrong. Being awesomer is easy if you believe everyone else wants to be awesomer too.

YOUR LIFESTYLE WAS AWESOMER

You partied 'til you passed out and lost your teeth while doing it. Life was about fun back then. There wasn't stress, money meant nothing, and you never had to cook your own meals. You were a child of leisure and every day was your vacation.

You were a skinny fat-ass with an inferno metabolism. You gorged yourself on all of life's delights and never gained a pound. Every meal was a belly-busting adventure where there was always room for dessert.

You're a living diet now. Your life is counted in calories and measured in waistline inches. You exercise for the lie that your body hasn't given up on you.

Life's too short to live it eating salad. Ice cream still rules, so let's accept a fat happy life rather than live a skinny miserable one. Let's recognize that our soft edges are part of kicking ass and living an awesomer life.

BEING CARRIED EVERYWHERE

You were an easily transportable ball of fat and snot that everyone wanted to take turns carrying. You lured in suckers with your cute looks and quickly turned them into your own personal Sherpas. You never walked a step in your life that you didn't want to take.

There's a reason they don't make adult-sized Baby Bjorns. Sorry, some things can't be that awesomer ever again.

WEARING WHATEVER YOU WANTED

You always dressed for the occasion, especially if that occasion was rolling hard in the streets, looking fresh, and hunting down adventure like a poacher of fun. Few people put it together better than you.

You're an oxford nightmare of normal now. On the sidewalk runway of life, you'd rather blend in than stand out.

Let's get back to dressing for the occasion of kicking ass and planning to live life so hard that we need to wear a helmet daily.

BRINGING THE THUNDER

You were a hangover's worst nightmare and sounded like musical Tourette's. Earplugs weren't enough to stop the auditory assault that you conducted. Every toy you owned hissed, banged, rang, or thumped to your delight and the hatred of everyone else.

Adulthood has quieted your chaos and brought you down to library-appropriate volume.

Let's turn it back up to 11 again. Bring on the noise complaints. The world needs our ruckus.

PASSING THE HELL OUT

You had the system beat before you ever knew it. Instead of groggily dragging your body through the day, you charged up your fury with every spare moment you could find.

Now naps are a sign of the lazy. A desk siesta could get you fired because society has a falsely skewed image of "productivity."

Those forty winks made us high-functioning balls of chaos ready to dominate the day. Instead of mainlining caffeine, let's shut it down for a bit so we can get turnt back up.

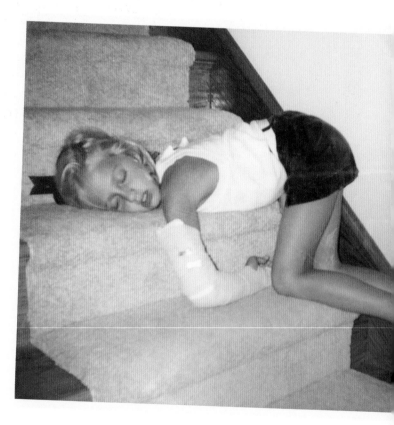

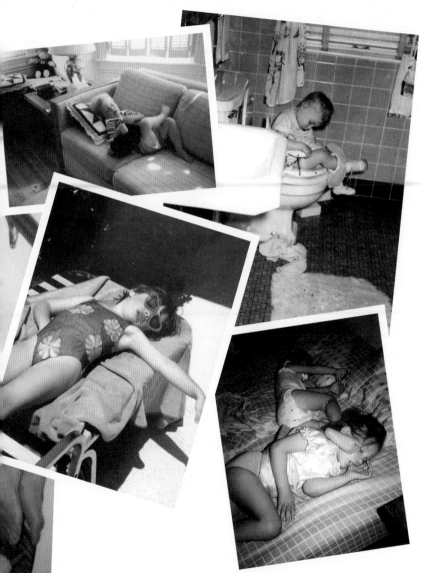

TASTING THE WORLD

You feared no germs and bravely savored the flavor of everything on earth. You'd taste dirt, dine on dog bones, and shit a rainbow nightmare of the crayons you ate. The world was your oyster, if oysters were what was in your mouth at that moment.

There's no adventure in your taste buds now. The spice of life is missing because you're afraid of all the delicacies you've never eaten.

Let's put our mouths in harm's way again. Let's find deliciously weird things and feast on foods we can't pronounce. Let's find the awesomer flavors again.

BEING A SUPERHERO

Back then you donned the uniform for that day's adventure. You could be a superhero, an army man, or anything else your sugar-fueled brain could conjure. Capes were part of your daily wardrobe and underwear was worn exclusively over your pants.

Now you're badged a Comic-Con nerd if you've broken free from the half-Windsor noose. Your capes collect dust until you can fly them on October 31st.

Dressing awesomer doesn't have to be one day a year. Let's fly an S under our suits and Clark Kent it up at work. Let's outerwear our underwear and be weekend superheroes like awesomer kids would.

You had more energy than a triple espresso Red Bull. You Super-manned off swings, surfed down slides, and played lava tag 'til you were dragged home. Those recess minutes were your time to live dangerously. You needed play because play is what made you feel alive.

Recess is forever over now. Playgrounds are for kids and you're herded into offices each day like white-collar cattle. You can't remember the last time you went to a jungle gym, or even a park for that matter.

Playgrounds spark creativity, keep us healthy, and plus, slides are dope. It's time to reclaim our recess and play outside again like when we were awesomer kids.

NOT GETTING UP TO GO

There are only two times in your life when it is socially acceptable to shit yourself mid-conversation, and you've already lived through one. You're going to have to wait 'til your golden years to be that awesome again.

DIGGING FOR TREASURE

The world was your Kleenex and you freely wiped freshly mined gold in every church, school, and house you encountered. You were a Banksy of boogers who left newly-picked graffiti on any surface within finger's reach. It was disgusting, but damn did it feel good.

You still pick your nose, don't lie. Good on you. Keep being an awesomer kid.

BEING FLEXIBLE

Contortionists cringed at the twisted positions into which you morphed your body. It was as if you had rubber bones and elastic muscles that never snapped under your strain. When you said you put your foot in your mouth it was always literal. Your flexibility was an evolutionary gift that saved you from injury each time you crash-test-dummied yourself through another day.

Now those once limber muscles have concrete-hardened and your joints are seizing up like rusty hinges.

We stretched as awesomer kids because we were active. Office chairs are killing us, so let's kill them. Let's stand up, run, play, and kick ass until our bodies are as indestructible as they used to be.

SIMPLE PLEASURES

Back when ADD was called "being a kid," you were ripping through life making everything fun. Sprinklers were water parks, bikes were daredevil machines, and bubbles were pure joy.

Now you can't see past your iPad and miss out on actual moments because you're too busy Instagramming them. You've stopped living in the moment and started living for "likes."

Let's power down the bullshit and get back to basics. Forts aren't going to build themselves and cardboard-roll sword fights aren't going to happen on their own. Let's go back to just enjoying the simple things again.

Your addiction to the white candy rush was rehab-level. You'd have ice cream for breakfast with a Skittles chaser if your parents let you. Cookie Monster was your worst influence and the reason your dentist got a new Porsche.

You've got sweet tooth guilt now and fat pants sadness. High-fructose fears have poisoned your love affair with candied goodness and doctors have robbed the fun out of the rush.

Crack out the cookie dough because it's time to party again. A candy bender every now and then never killed a man. There's a reason they say success tastes so sweet.

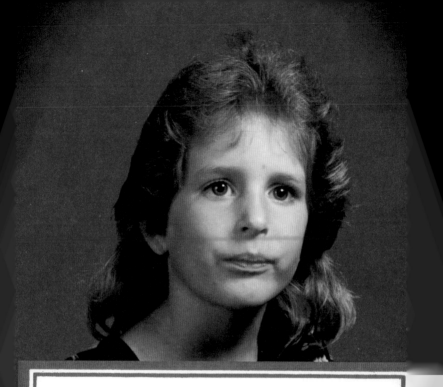

THE WORST HAIRCUTS

School up front and recess in the back, your butchered locks were an experiment in expressing yourself. Luckily, kids' memories last as long as their attention spans and your hairtastrophe was forgotten like yesterday's sack lunch.

You won't risk it now. You fear the pictures on social media. Life is calculated down to the strand and "nothing drastic" is the first thing that leaves your lips.

Let's get wild again. Let's invent new versions of mullets and shave random parts of our heads. Let's put our hair in harm's way because after all, it always grows back, unlike your awesomeness.

TWO-WHEELED TERROR

Bombing hills like a hell rider on wheels, you cruised at death speed with a white-knuckled grip. Sweet jumps, wicked-ass wheelies, and dope skid-stops were the mad skills you terrorized the streets with.

You've given up your wheels now and traded them in for a cage. Your life is a cruise control of adulthood.

Four wheels make you fat, two wheels make you awesomer. So let's dust off the seat and grease up the chain for trouble. After all, the sunset isn't going to ride off into itself.

FIVE-SECOND RULE? BULLSHIT.

Your clumsy little meat fists couldn't hold onto anything, which is why your buffet was eaten off a linoleum plate. Some seek the spice of life, but you realized long ago that it was found on the floor.

Now each amazing morsel of food that falls on the floor is fearfully thrown away. You have a Lysol-drenched life and keep hand sanitizer on your keychain. Your immune system has forgotten how to fight. Think of all the delicious crumbs you've missed out on.

What doesn't kill you makes you awesomer, so let's eat off the floor again. Let's make our immune systems bulletproof by tasting all that life has to offer and then some.

Your jumpsuit for destruction kicked ass harder than steel-toed boots. Once zipped to your chin, you went on one last terror lap around the house before passing out.

You look the way giving up feels and your sad PJs bum out your dreams.

Let's kick it old school and rock footie PJs so hard that we win at dreaming. They're still the dopest thing since ice cream and, lucky you, they come in adult sizes now.

DANGEROUS TOYS

Back then you had deadly playthings. There weren't parental warnings on them because these instruments of destruction weren't designed for your little hands. But entrusted to your care, you learned responsibility while somehow managing not to kill yourself.

Now life is a bland existence of safety scissors that don't even cut paper and nontoxic paste that has no flavor when you eat it.

Screw that. Darwin was right and life should be survival of the fittest. If you're dumb enough to get hurt doing something, don't sue because you'll ruin the fun for the rest of us trying to be awesomer again.

CLEANING THE BOWL

The leftover bits of uncooked delicacies that clung to kitchen tools were the sweetest part of being a kid. It was blasphemy to dare wash away such gold when you had a perfectly capable mouth-dishwasher. While you weren't a culinary expert, it did seem foolish to bother baking what already tasted like success.

Our hearts still skip a beat when the blender stops, and cookie dough still tastes best when it's raw. We may have grown up, but this never stopped being awesomer.

WINNING EVERYTHING

Face it, you were shitty at everything. But despite your inabilities, you had kryptonite cuteness that had foes throwing in the towel because they felt terrible beating a kid. So each "W" on your championship belt laid a confident foundation for you to keep kicking life's ass.

Now life hits back and you beat yourself up harder than your opponents do. Your belief in yourself is shattered by doubt, and sweatpants feel more comfortable than trying does.

Let's get our title back of being a badass. Instead of giving up, let's get better. Instead of saying we can't, let's keep trying 'til we can, and hold our awesomer hands high as champions of living.

FULL THROTTLE

You screamed at death speed across this earth in a reckless race of adrenaline chasing. Alive was the feeling you pursued at chaos-miles-per-hour. Your parents tried to govern the speed at which you could live, but there was never any limit that could be set on your life.

You're stuck in the slow lane now. Your lead foot is made of feathers because you fear reaching the reaper at the red line.

It's time to stop living leisurely and hammer the gas. Open roads are calling our souls to speed because slow will never feel as alive as fast.

BEING IN SHAPE

You were a Greek god of gifted physical capabilities. Walking? No. You lived your life at a full sprint and ran household marathons each day.

You've got a Jell-O backside now and bacon strip love handles. You get winded when forced to take stairs instead of the elevator.

Let's get back in awesomer shape. How are we going to conquer the world if we're creating an ass print in the couch? Let's run everywhere again, because life isn't lived sitting still.

GETTING PAID FOR CHORES

Your cash hustle used to be much easier than a nine to five. For a couple bucks each week, you were given simple household labors: dusting, filling the dishwasher, and not living in your own filth. Your parents paid you under the table and your weekly allowance was enough to make it rain at the candy store.

Nobody is going to pay you to clean your own bedroom now. You're your own Mr. Clean and those Scrubbing Bubbles bastards aren't pulling their weight. When a long hard day of adulthood ends, a house full of chores is usually waiting.

At this point, your only options are having an awesomer kid of your own to do your dirty work, or sucking it up and making the best of it. Sorry.

Stay gold.

BIG WHEEL GANGS

Screw training wheels. You were a three-wheeled badass and a drifting legend of the suburban streets. You and your crew of half-pint Hell's Angels were the envy of every kid stuck kicking rocks on the block. It wasn't just a toy, it was a status symbol, and the reason lemonade stands popped up in front of every house that didn't have one.

Puberty outsized you for your fly ride, but could never erase the memories of sliding that beast sideways down a hill. You may ride two wheels now, but three will always have your heart.

PLAYING IN SPRINKLERS

When summer was in full hellfire mode, these rainmakers were a momentary escape from the sauna that had become your existence. You soaked in every moment and didn't give a shit about having wet hair.

Now you avoid sprinklers because you don't want to get your iPhone wet. You'd rather trudge through the thick heat and wallow in your sweat stains than catch a moment of relief.

Summer's too fun to be miserable. Let's hide bathing suits under our suits and get soaked like the day will never end.

LETTING IT ALL HANG OUT

Back when your shit barely swung, you knew pants were evil leg traps created by society to break your free spirit. Why print Superman, Batman, Transformers, or Alf on your whitey tighties if the world wasn't going to see them? Decency be damned, hanging out in your skid rows was a Friday night tradition and a Saturday morning cartoon institution.

Now you don't want to be the weird guy in his underwear. You fear being judged more than you care to be comfortable. Why?

The awesomer version of you never cared what people thought. All he cared about was doing whatever was comfortable, and sometimes that was letting it all hang out. So go for it.

You could pop, lock, and drop fresh moves to any beat. When the rhythm gripped you by the Huggies, you answered the call and showed the world how you got down.

Now you're a stiff board when the beat drops. You awkwardly fumble along looking like a stickman having a seizure. So, you sit on the outskirts of the dance floor while everyone else tears it up.

It's time to throw down again when our jam comes on. Let's be possessed by the music and let the rhythm move us just like an awesomer kid would.

SUGARY CEREAL

Each morning was a marshmallow dream of puffed pops swimming in sugary milk. Breakfast was candy and each box came with buried treasures. When you were done slurping down the last drops, it was time to go out and prove that you put the champion in breakfast of champions.

Now your day begins with organic, gluten-free, sugar-free, fun-free bowls of bullshit. Your buried treasure is health benefits now and breakfast is the saddest meal of the day.

Well, screw that. Who says you can't indulge in some overly-processed breakfast gold with a cartoon character on the front? Those bowls of deliciousness made you into the awesomer kid you were, so maybe you should stop playing by every rule and start your day off right.

GETTING HIGH

These kid-catapults were your chance to grab some sky and soar like a superhero. They turned an average backyard into a neighborhood hangout. They were an insurance nightmare, but you lived on the line of danger and were determined to double-bounce your way into the history books.

Now you've got a bore-yard. Instead of making a fun zone, you have a perfectly groomed landscape to raise your property value.

We need to get high again—by jumping, that is. Trampolines don't cost the bajillions of dollars we once thought they did. Let's reach for the heavens and bounce our way back to being awesomer. (And it's great exercise too, if you need an adult rationalization.)

CLIMBING TREES

Your other mother was nature and you were best friends with her woodland children. They were hideouts and lookouts that allowed you to oversee your child-sized kingdom. Every block had an unscalable monster, but your pint-sized lumberjack pride refused to let you give up until you fell at least once.

You've turned over a new leaf now and stopped trying to ascend to the highest heights. A forest of challenges sits at your doorstep and you can't even see the adventure in it.

The best views in the neighborhood aren't through your windows, and spying on your neighbors is a little more thrilling when you feel like Rambo. Let's get some sap on our hands again like awesomer kids would and watch the sunset from somewhere higher than ground level.

ZUBAZ

The playground had never seen swag like yours. When other kids were still stuck in their stonewashed phase, you arrived looking fresh to death in your tiger stripes. It was game over on fashion and every time you Hammer-danced down the street all the kids knew . . . "Can't touch this."

You're as adventurous as khakis now. Your lame legs can't handle the fresh prints they once wore.

No amount of wishing will ever allow you to rock Zubaz that hard again. It was a moment in time that will never repeat itself, so be thankful you were at least awesomer when it happened.

EATING DIRT

You lived by the motto, "God made dirt and dirt don't hurt." Soap got soiled from touching your grimy mitts, and no amount of detergent could clean the battle scars on your outfits. Puddles needed to be stomped in, and mud pies needed to be made.

You're living a crisp linen life in a Tide To-Go world. You look down your clean nose at the dirtier parts of society and obsessively avoid soiling any part of your existence.

Clean is boring; being a dirty awesomer kid is fun. So let's kick up some dirt, roll down a hill, and grass-stain our way into a good time again.

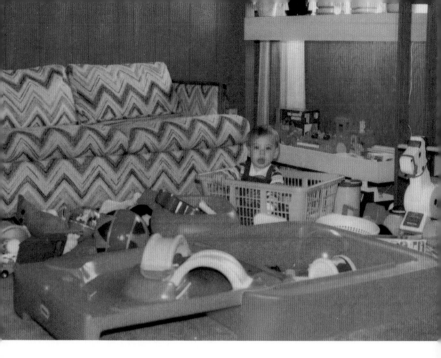

HAVING A CRAP-TON OF TOYS

You were a Toys "R" Us kid with a Taj Mahal playroom. You filled those four walls with your imagination and those molded bits of entertainment were your best friends. Life looked like all fun and games back then, but you were becoming a baby Einstein and these were the learning tools.

Your once great collection has been donated now. Action figures and miniature cars are considered immature, so you left childish things where you thought they belonged, in the past.

There's no such thing as being too old for toys. Legos were the shit, and they still are. Peter Pan had it right all along: let's never grow up.

Your fresh prints were the only thing more bitching sweet than you. A yelling shark wearing shades and diving out of a Technicolor tiger-print background? Hell yeah, sign you up. You were a neon icon that scream-punched the world in the face with your shirts and showed everyone what "wildlife" really meant.

Now you're another bland-colored pocket-T in the sad Hanes collection of life. Instead of being printed with glorious images, your lame shirts are printed with nothing.

Let's high-step it into history wearing shirts as awesome as we are. Who says adults can't wear tiger shirts or show up at a party rocking dinosaurs on our chests?

NINJA SKILLZ

You were a Ninja-Turtle-trained killer who could sweep the leg better than any Karate Kid. Your fists were semi-lethal weapons trained from hours of TV in your living room dojo. There wasn't a #2 pencil you couldn't snap because you had a bathrobe black belt in kung fu fury.

You don't know Jean-Claude Van Damme about hand-to-hand combat now. Your judo chop is soft, and your roundhouse has no kick. Instead of practicing the moves from movies, you've gone all rom-com weak.

Clear out the garage and bring out the boards because it's time to get awesomer again. When that next *Blood Sport* marathon hits TV, you better start hitting back.

MOMENTS THAT WERE AWESOMER

All moments in life aren't created equal.
Birthdays were the greatest thing since
Christmas and summer vacation lasted
forever. Along the way we lost our snow
days and Disney World became a creepy
place for us to visit. But just because
we can't count our age on our fingers
anymore doesn't mean that we have to
give up the moments that made being a
kid awesomer.

PARTYING

You were built to rage. Inside your tiny body were all the best traits of a partying great. You could burp with the best of them. You could puke like the worst of them. And no night ended 'til you pissed your pants after passing out.

Now you're too tired to get turned up. Netflix and a nice night in are your wild times and you've got too much to do to be hungover.

It's time to tap back into the awesomer spirit that would have made you a legend of wild nights out. Instead of staying in after sunset, let's get no sleep 'til sunrise. After all, the best stories never start with "I decided to stay in."

SQUIRT GUN FIGHTS

It's a tough life on the suburban streets. Unless you're packing a pistol full of water bullets, you get soaked. Epic battles with Big Wheel drive-bys were common on your block, which is why you never left the stoop without enough H_2O in your soak-piece to wet a fool if he stepped out of line.

Now anything shaped like a gun will get you in trouble. You can't even point your fingers without stirring rage in some anti-fun group that is trying to instill fear into this once great nation of Super Soakers.

But it's just water, and squirt guns were one of the best parts of being a kid. Let's reclaim being awesomer by spraying anyone who dares try to stop our fun.

BATH TIME

In your bathroom-sized indoor pool, you splish-splashed off your filth. It was a No More Tears good time where wet mohawks were always in fashion and bubbles were the best thing invented since animal crackers.

Now you quickly hose yourself down in the shower. Scrubbing off the day is less about enjoyment and more about speed, just like everything else in life.

Don't grow out of the tub. Grab life by the rubber ducky and jump back into soaking up suds. You have to get clean anyway—why not at least make it an awesomer experience each time you do?

TV

Those moving pictures were your snake charmer and mesmerized you into a standstill. When your eyes were glued in, it was one of the few moments when you weren't raining destruction throughout the house. It was an electronic babysitter that gave your parents some peace.

Now TV is considered a waste of time that systematically melts your intelligence. It's a boob tube that locks you into an ass-print on the couch for marathon sessions of watching whole seasons at once.

But you know what? Who cares? Let's shut down our brains like when we were awesomer and zone into some zoning out. Relaxing is an important part of life too and we shouldn't forget it.

PHOTOBOMBING

The other little angels of this world posed perfectly, but you were Satan's son, and a problem child of unbridled chaos. Your parents told you your face would stay that way, which you thought was perfect.

Now you smile politely and show a socially-predetermined appropriate amount of teeth. You're just another random guy to forget in every photo ever taken of you.

Screw being a background character in everyone else's memories. Let's steal the show again like when we were awesomer kids and go down in portrait history as the goofballs we were born to be.

MISSING TEETH

Four out of five dentists couldn't tell you anything. Why brush your teeth when they'll fall out anyway? You were always an accident away from a payday because your bankroll was stuck in your gums. And nothing said you were from the tough part of the playground like two missing front teeth.

Now, a tooth falling out will wreck your life. Flossing, bleaching, scrubbing, polishing, and check-ups: every action is a careful attempt to maintain what you used to so carelessly stuff under your pillow.

Screw that. Imperfection is beautiful. The most interesting people you'll ever meet are the ones with messed-up teeth. So hang on to your imperfections and kick shit like an awesomer kid 'til the end.

BEING CUTE

Those chubby cheeks could get you away with more murders than O.J. Simpson's lawyers. You were a walking pile of dirty with a poo-filled diaper and still straight melted hearts with your puppy eyes.

Now you hide your natural cute. Each morning is a calculated procedure with makeup lies and hair-dyed deception.

Let's face it, unless you Marty McFly your way back, you'll never be that a-damn-dorable again. But gaining age gains wisdom and there's beauty in that too. Let's accept the gray and love the lines and make growing old be awesomer.

CARDBOARD BOXES

Your sugar-fueled imagination turned garbage into hours of fun. Boxes were race cars that traveled to outer space and nap castles when you were tired. Those corrugated dream machines took you to places acid couldn't take adults.

Now they're just forgotten gems easily discarded with yesterday's waste. But what if we looked at them again with the same wonder our younger eyes had? What could we build?

Let's reclaim the fun of being awesomer kids again and start making shit with the most amazing material known to man: cardboard boxes.

POWER WHEELS

Only the badassest kid on the block cruised in these dope whips. They may have only had a top speed that even an asthmatic kid could outrun, but they still drove envy into the hearts of your neighbors.

Now our transportation is more functional than fun. We're another fuel-efficient car in the traffic jam of life.

Let's get back to being the envy of the block. We can trade in our sad sedans for adventure wheels. Let's feel the wind whip through our hair and make the neighborhood jealous of our awesomer rides again.

SPLASHING CARES AWAY

When the thermostat of summer was stuck on full broil, you headed for the oasis of splash where you could slide your worries away. It was a wonderland of waterfalls and wading pools where you didn't just beat the heat, you kicked its ass.

You look at pools like they're public piss puddles now. Screaming and splashing ruin your "quiet time" in the sun.

Screw that. When the heat is blasting, let's make our own water parks. Tarps are cheap and inflatable pools make great landing zones. Let's slip and slide our way into being awesomer again and show summer she can still kiss our sunburnt backsides.

RESCUING PETS

You were raised barefoot by Mother Nature. The lost children of her woods were quickly adopted into your pint-sized wolf pack. Your eyes were unblinded to those in need and you poured out your tiny heart to help them.

Now your pets are carefully bred and carry Louis Vuitton price tags. You tote them around like a fashion statement and try to get insta-famous for their cute looks.

Let's go back to helping out the strays of the animal kingdom. Instead of wasting money buying a best friend, let's be awesomer again by adopting one.

With only a pinch full of pride, you threw off the world's rules with your clothes. You were all about kicking it in your skin-suit and letting your dice roll. The world knew exactly what kind of man you were, and even though it wasn't much, you were never ashamed.

Now you hide under your clothes and laws keep you trapped in them. You fear baring it all because you worry about what people might think. Magazines shame you into self-hate and models distort your reality.

You were given what you got and you can't change who you are— so screw it, be proud of it. Show it off, accept it, and start living again.

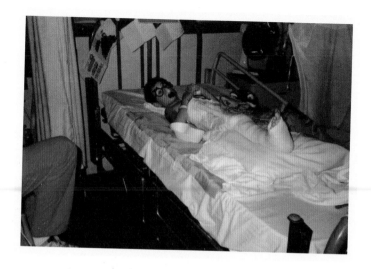

BROKEN BONES

When you live at full throttle, eventually something has to break. Steel couldn't withstand the sheer force of your aggression, and neither could your bones. Casts were trophies of pushing your life to the extreme. You took it in stride—even if you couldn't stride—because the bar of badassery got set a little bit higher.

The wind isn't full of the caution you've thrown into it now. It's a safety-first lifestyle where risk takes a backseat.

The most alive moment anyone can have is dancing on the line of destruction. You knew that as an awesomer kid. Let's go back to finding our breaking point and discovering how it feels when your adrenaline is cranked to 11.

CARNIVAL CHAOS

These traveling festivals were a summer highlight that wrecked your life with a fun hangover. Sometime between the corn dog lunch, cotton candy high, petting zoo germs, and tilt-a-whirl puke, you had the time of your small life.

Now you see these germ-filled, freak show factories for the traveling nightmare that they actually are. The magic has washed away to show the danger in every ride and you look down your nose at the deep-fried delicacies.

But why? Throw off the shackles of adulthood and indulge in an elephant ear. Get your face painted and forget that the games are all rigged just like an awesomer kid would. It can be fun again, if you want it to be.

Some things will always be awesomer.

GETTING SICK

Feeling bad never felt so good. For those glorious days under the weather, you lived like a king among kids. All your life's desires were delivered to your bedside in an endless Popsicle dream where the price was always right.

Now your job doesn't care how shitty you feel, you still have to come in. You bargain with your immune system as you wish for death in each wheezy breath.

Let's call off work instead of complaining the whole day through it. Bosses don't give out Purple Hearts, so don't contaminate the office. The couch is calling your inner awesomer kid and the reruns need to be watched.

In the endless weekend where Sunday never comes, you lived as King Shit under the sun. It was funemployment at its finest as you literally didn't do a damn thing for three whole months.

Summer is broken now. You sit in an office and cry into memos as you watch the long days of warmth slip away outside. There's no vacation from your brain and the weekend always ends too quickly.

It's time to flip the desk. Screw being caged into A/C and waking up one day only to realize it's winter. Let's refill our souls by soaking up some sun like awesomer kids would. Work can wait.

HALLOWEEN

For one day a year you terrorized the suburbs with candy demands and pitied the fool who dared give you an apple. It was Christmas for your sweet tooth when you collected a diabetic-shock-inducing level of fun-sized sugar. At the end of the night you sorted your treasure and systematically made terrible trades with younger, dumber siblings to screw them out of their best treats. Your pillowcase haul was a point of pride that proved you were the king of trick or treat.

No one wants to give you candy now. But you get dressed up for drinking and still celebrate this amazing day in a new adult way. Good on you, way to stay awesomer.

WINTER

When it felt like hell had frozen over, it was just the right temperature for fun. Epic snowball battles, saucer sled sliding, and forts made for frozen royalty. You were living in the snow globe of life and had millions of possibilities of things to do.

Now the cold is our curse. It aggravates our commutes and locks into our bones. Each day we drag ourselves through the slush of life desperately waiting for warm.

Let's kick Old Man Winter's ass again. Instead of hiding inside, let's make the most of the worst. Complaining about winter only makes it last longer, so let's make it awesomer by enjoying every flake of it.

CHRISTMAS

Each year Santa would slide his jolly fat ass down the chimney and make it rain under the tree. And as you anxiously tore hell through the paper, you shit yourself with excitement as your wildest dreams came true. This day was the benchmark of happiness to which all other days in life were compared.

'Tis the season of stress now. You give thoughtless gift cards and drown your liver in liquid holiday cheer as you struggle your way through family get-togethers. Your Christmas cheer is like Santa . . . fake.

Since egg-nogging ourselves unconscious isn't healthy, let's make it the best day of our lives again. Buy an uglier sweater, accept the chaos, throw another Yule log on the fire, and ho ho hold down the holidays like an awesomer kid would.

There's a reason "wild child" is a term and "wild adult" isn't.

NEW YEAR'S RESOLUTIONS

After throwing deuces to another year of killing it, you stared down the next 365 with mother-effin' game changer plans. You were going to be the Michael Jordan of potty training, the Bob Ross of finger paints, and the Leonardo da Vinci of Legos. It was a mission of fun where every day's plan was to play 'til you passed out.

You've gone soft now. When the ball drops, you kiss enjoying yourself goodbye. No more staying out late, eating double-deep-fried amazing-ness, or sleeping in until the sun sets. You've resolved yourself to limit the good times instead of deciding to make shit happen.

Forget played-out resolutions. Let's make this year about jumping out of planes, chasing down life, and being a total badass like when we were an awesomer kid. There are 365 new bullets in the gun; let's go have some fun.

Instead of growing older, let's grow awesomer.

WATER WINGS

Cannonball, bitches! With flip-flops flopping and sunblock blocking, you owned the water with your wings. Every end was the deep end as you won at summer with your swim swagger and doggie-paddle dopeness.

Now you've given up your inflatable badassery. Your poolside accessories are for vanity only and you're determined to show off your athleticism in the pool.

But floating is a lazy man's paradise. Let's whip out our floaties again and strut with pride knowing that we don't have to lift a finger to stay afloat.

YOUR FIRST CRUSH

She was your kindergarten princess and the only one you'd share your pudding pack with. Playdates in the park were the best part of your week and no candy bar got you as high as her love did. It was a simpler, more innocent time, until she broke your heart for that Canadian boy who moved in down the street.

You're a jaded mess now who has more baggage than an airport. You've handed your heart out a million times and have always gotten it back in pieces.

Keep falling. The kid with his heart on his sleeve is still inside you and looking for that first crush feeling again. Look everywhere 'til you find it again (except maybe not on the playground anymore). Your awesomer other half is waiting to be found.

HATING GROWN-UP EVENTS

They always began with the same speech: "You better be on your best behavior." Those few words were enough to throw you into a tornado-sized temper tantrum because the next few hours of your life were going to be a boring hell of being paraded around like the angel you weren't. Seconds felt like hours and each minute your dress clothes slowly suffocated your spirit out of your body.

Admit it: adult events are still the bane of your existence. The small talk hangs in the air with an awkward tension and you spend the whole night carefully plotting your Irish goodbye.

We can't be volun-told to attend now. Let's RSVP "See you never" and spend our time doing something dope instead. We're in charge now. Only we can make the choice to be awesomer or not.

HAVING A SIBLING

You were going to wreck that kid's life by teaching him all the terrible little things your warped mind had discovered while running wild on a candy bender. He was going to be your crash test dummy and personal punching bag. Nothing was going to separate you other than the years you were older than him.

Like two ships in the night, you've gently drifted away from your siblings. Work, priorities, distance, and other bullshit excuses have made you more like acquaintances than kin.

Don't forget the hand-me-down DNA you share with your awesomer other half. You grew up together and that's no excuse to grow apart. So why not meet at your parents' place and trash it for old times' sake like you did as awesomer kids?

PEEING IN POOLS

When it was go time, you went. It was the only moment in life you could be a piss-pants and get away with it. That little warm patch of yellow heaven was your way of heating the water around you. You enjoyed the pool a bit too much, and if everyone knew how many times you turned their swimming hole into your giant toilet, you'd be banned for life.

BIRTHDAYS

For 365 days you chased death, kissed danger, and outlived logical life expectancies. That's why on the unholy anniversary of your shit-kicking arrival everyone treated you like a god to celebrate your survival of another year. It was a sugar orgy of frosted cartoon characters and the endless ice cream sundae of your dreams.

Now you get generic half-honest social media birthday wishes and crappy gift cards. The celebration is gone and you drown your birthday with shots of tequila bought by friends at a sad happy hour.

But why not go big again? We should make it a "me" day and do only the dopest shit of our dreams. Ice cream for breakfast and no work 'til tomorrow. Let's buy ourselves the presents we want and ring in one more year of us by being awesomer again.

CONCLUSION

You're the adult now. It's your choices you have to live with. You can fade quietly into the sunset of your life to leave a legacy of endless workdays, home improvement weekends, and stories so bland that even you fall asleep thinking about them.

Or . . .

Starting today you can be the awesomer version of you again. Stay out later, live a little harder, chase your dreams, drink more, eat whatever the hell you please, break rules, and when it all ends, die a legend.

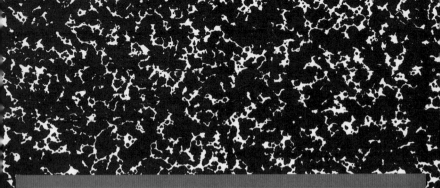

THANK YOU

All of the success of this book belongs to the awesomer kids inside of it. Without you being a pint-sized badass back in the day, this book could never have existed. Thank you for being part of this project; I'm truly grateful to all of you.

To Michelle, thank you being part of my life, part of this book, and for being there during the crazy process that was writing this book. I couldn't have done this without you.

To all my friends, thank you for sending me your photos and sharing your stories of how you were awesomer.

To Chronicle Books, thank you for believing in this idea and believing in me.

CREDITS

Front cover photo: Lane Jordan

Page 4: Matt and Brad Getty

Page 7: Hanna Choi

Page 8: Eric Cislo

Page 9: Rebecca Brown

Page 10: Lirra Schiebler

Page 11: Vince Fergus

Page 12: Emma Walsh

Page 14: Courtney Smith

Page 15: Brad Getty

Page 16: Ruth George

Page 17: Sarah "Snorton" Norton

Page 18: Georgia Sheales

Page 19: Joe Michael Reyes

Page 20: Matthew McFerrin

Page 21: Vanessa Gauvin-Brodeur

Page 22: Tim Eichlin

Page 23: Jeff Gonick

Page 24: Aaron Davis

Page 25: Marie-Laurence Grenier-Trempe

Page 26: Eddie Leffler

Page 28: Katerie Fiset

Page 29: Zack Belmonte

Page 30: Hanna Choi

Page 31: Ceil Mattingly

Page 32: Brian Moss

Page 33: Michael Chase

Page 34: Victoria Thomas

Page 35: Shawna Gibbs Photography

Page 36: Ben Johannemann

Page 38: Sam Mehrathon

Page 39: Barry Stark

Page 40: Lane Jordan

Page 42: Samuel Heart

Page 43: Katie Blackerby

Page 44: Everett Ching

Page 45: Maria Sedjo

Page 46: Fiona Skinner

Page 47: Rachel Ryan Douglass

Page 48: Katy Alambo

Page 49: Jamie Gurnell

Page 51: Katerie Fiset

Page 52: Rachel Lewis

Page 53: Monte Miller

Page 54: Dylan Johnson

Page 55: Eddie Leffler

Page 56: Kendall Beveridge

Page 57: Larry Getty, Katerie Fiset, Jim Cunningham, Joey Prochnow

Page 58: Stacie Getty

Page 59: Rachael Donnelly

Page 60: Danielle Eck, Guillaume Vasseur, Brad and Matt Getty

Page 62: Maria Noel Diaz

Page 63: Eddie Leffler

Page 64: Lily Landes

Page 65: Jamie Flam

Page 67: Kenny Flannery

Page 68: Ian Kennedy

Page 69: Jes Voight

Page 70: Eric Cislo

Page 72: Barry Stark